"Kerrin McCadden is haunted by her family's migration from Ireland ('Hold a wake for the living, the leaving') and tells a very American story in *American Wake*, a textured story of loss and gain, of what she calls 'prodigal ghosts,' the Old World and the New World, too, the broken family patched together, somehow sustained, ongoing. This book slows things down that are speeding past and wakes us up to the past and present tense. I love its worried wakefulness."

—Edward Hirsch, author of *Stranger by Night*

"When Irish myths harmonize with the voices of a real family—is it a murmur or a din? A song or a haunting? The sea is a place terrifyingly large and deep and yet familiar, for inside the self is a kind of sea—a beloved brother can drown there. A sister can call for him for years. There is a paper-thin ridge between the sea-land of the dead and the land-sea of the living, and it's on that ridge that poet McCadden rides, writes, shouts into the wind. Not a banshee—a storyteller. A sister, a daughter, a self who can begin to see how the waves lap and overlap life, grief, memory. This book doesn't warn as much as warm—it keeps company, shares the complexity of loving one another. McCadden's voice is synesthetic (sense-mixing) and textural, atmospheric. Then she gathers ether and nerves together to a sharp point with which she etches her lines (lineal, liminal lifelines) inscribing a family she can't quite write back to life, but she can tell them, tell of them, see them, and, most intimately, let us see them in her."

—Brenda Shaughnessy, author of *The Octopus Museum*

"Contrasting the luscious femininities of a Tess Gallagher in her peregrinations from Washington to Sligo with the stern abrasions of a Seamus Heaney translating himself from Station Island to Harvard, Kerrin McCadden's *American Wake* explores in depth the repercussions of emigration from generation to tragic generation, at one point receding as far back as Cuchulain."

—Medbh McGuckian, author of *Marine Cloud Brightening*

"The core of Kerrin McCadden's music is a purifying sound that ritualizes grief but also posits joy and curiosity as vested markers of living fully in the face of difficult times. McCadden is a storyteller as much as a singer. *American Wake* navigates loss, no doubt, but with such unparalleled sensitivity and inventiveness that language becomes its own jubilant force of survival. A reader will find instructive the profound care and assuredness by which she handles family stories and shared memories that border on a kind holiness of singing and a shaping of sacred narratives."

—Major Jackson, author of *The Absurd Man*

"'I think finding anything in the sea/would be impossible. I am not at sea,' writes Kerrin McCadden at the beginning of her second book. 'I have lost everything here.' This is indeed a watery world, from New England's rivers and lakes to the Atlantic across which her ancestors escaped famine, a world where McCadden's singular speaker must start over again, as they did. This is a world of myth: in her retelling of Cuchulain, the Irish giant protects the speaker even as he self-destructs, and the speaker becomes a selkie in order to find oblivion, albeit a temporary one, from the difficulty of human connection. In *American Wake*, a husband is given an aubade featuring a paving company; a brother dies again and again; and the rivers, lakes and seas seamlessly connect us to other worlds: rural life, Ireland, our younger selves, the underworld. These are sustaining poems, a gift in our times."

—Connie Voisine, author of *The Bower*

"The poems in this powerful, haunted book won't let go of the grief they carry, because the deepest current here is to honor the dead, to find the purpose and dignity of those lost to history, to domestic fracture, to addiction. Ironically, the burden leads the poet to look under every stone in an effort to resist the feeling that such loss is inevitable, a cruel fate we can't avoid. Touching the stones, however, directs the aching sweep of this book, and doing so, the poet spans place, time, and experience to make a home, suspended above all that is unknown and unknowable. This is a book that passes through the valley of the shadow of death to arrive at wisdom and love, and implies there is no other way to go."

—Maurice Manning, author of *Railsplitter*

"Kerrin McCadden is a poet who knows things—about islands and hills; about wandering and home; about moths and hawks and maps and trees; about nosing undersea cables across the Atlantic; the world as it looks from the Wayside Diner—and *American Wake* is her American sublime: poems for our elegiac now, built for all time. This is a stunning work."

—Joshua Jelly-Schapiro, author of *Island People*

Also by Kerrin McCadden

Landscape with Plywood Silhouettes
Keep This to Yourself

AMERICAN WAKE

AMERICAN
KERRIN

WAKE

poems

McCADDEN

Black Sparrow Press | Boston | 2021

First published in 2021 by BLACK SPARROW PRESS

GODINE
Boston, Massachusetts
godine.com

LIBRARY OF CONGRESS CATALOGING-IN-PUBLICATION DATA
Names: McCadden, Kerrin, author.
Title: American wake / Kerrin McCadden.
Description: Boston : Black Sparrow Press, 2021.
Identifiers: LCCN 2020042660 (print) | LCCN 2020042661 (ebook)
ISBN 9781574232479 (paperback)
ISBN 9781574232486 (ebook)
Subjects: LCGFT: Poetry.
Classification: LCC PS3613.C325 A84 2021 (print) | LCC PS3613.C325
   (ebook) | DDC 811/.6--dc23
LC record available at https://lccn.loc.gov/2020042660
LC ebook record available at https://lccn.loc.gov/2020042661

Cover Design: Rachel Willey

FIRST PRINTING, 2021
Printed in Canada

For Cliff

Contents

On all the beaches of the living world,
the shadows of where you were
are washed away by the tides.

—Ruth Stone

Epistle: Leaving

Dear train wreck, dear terrible engines, dear spilled freight,
      dear unbelievable mess, all these years later I think
      to write back. I was not who I am now. A sail is a boat,
      a bark is a boat, a mast is a boat, and the train was you and me.
      Dear dark, dear paper, dear files I can't toss, dear calendar
      and visitation schedule, dear hello and goodbye.
If a life is one thing and then another; if no grasses grow
      through the tracks; if the train wreck is a red herring;
      if goodbye then sincerely. Dear disappeared bodies
      and transitions, dear edge of a good paragraph.
      Before the wreck, we misunderstood revision.
I revise things now. I teach pertinence. A girl in class told
      us about some boys who found bodies on the tracks
      then went back and they were gone, the bodies.
      It was true that this story was a lie, like all things
done to be seen. I still think about this story, what it would
      be like to be a boy finding bodies out in the woods,
      however they were left—and think of all the ways they
      could be left. There I was, teaching the building
      of a good paragraph, dutiful investigator
of sentences, thinking dear boys, dear stillness in the woods,
      until, again, there is the boy I knew as a man
      whose father left him at a gas station, and unlike the lie
      of the girl's story, this one is true—he left him there for good.
Sometimes this boy, nine and pale, is sitting next to me, sitting there
      watching trains go past the gas station in Wyoming,
      thinking there is a train going one way, and a train
      going the other way, each at different and variable speeds:
      how many miles before something happens
      that feels like answers when we write them down—

like solid paragraphs full of transitional phrases
　　　and compound, complex sentences, the waiting space
　　　between things that ends either in pleasure or pain. He
　　　keeps showing up, dear boy, man now, and beautiful
like the northern forest, hardwoods iced over.

On the Moon

In my moon house, things were attached to the walls.
There were buttons I could push—cupboards opened
to release pillows, hermetically sealed meals, a deck of cards
—you should have seen them fly around! When I lived
on the moon, everything was safety engineered
in the home I built there. There are an equal number
of moon seas for joy and sadness, and I visited them each
in turn, as one would, wanting to stay whole in a life
governed as it was by outside forces, as if he were
more than one force—a man to face every day,
rocketing home just before he did. The moon was simple,
gray, like I imagined the world should be—simple
like the worn clapboards of a farmhouse, just a few
hardwood tables and chairs, a world where nothing falls
out of place and the only harsh words come because
something has been broken. How many times can someone
try to open a door when it's latched before the door is gouged
by the shoving, the wood pinched against the metal shank?
There is something fearful about the life expectancy of a door.
There were days when the dinner still needed salt,
days when the list was failed, days when one more thing
was my fault—how, anyway, could I have done x?
Some days I visited the seas: Sea of Nectar, Sea of Vapor.
Mornings, or what looked like mornings, I went walking
and painted landscapes from memory, the colors glaucous,
cinerous, cosmic latte, titanium white: gesso in layers on top,
scratched off with hobby screwdrivers I had on board,
each day a new array of craters, rilles, geographies I missed
back on earth, a planet less predictably territoried,
where I used to study doors, wait behind them, walk my finger
along roads of earlywood and latewood, study knots and wait,
sometimes, until I had it all traced before coming back out.

Seal Bride

Having stolen back my skin, I lub across rocks,
slip into water—my closable nostrils,
my closable ears. No one can tell me

what to do here. I welter and lumber
in all directions, fusiform—my flippers like wings.
I may be a fallen angel, or my brother may be,

I don't know. First I am thinking, and then
I am not. First I am remembering,
and then I am eating a fish, my sharp teeth mine.

Below, veins of telecommunications cable
I have no need for—no emails of mine
going anywhere anymore, a few maybe

trying to find me. I go down. Above, the sky
a shiny toy—a building set of tinsel and sequins
knocked down through the sea. I can go anywhere,

push away with my hind flippers and press
my nose forward, skyward, corkscrew-ward.
You know what I will say next. It is easy

to forget why I came here. It is easy to forget
why I left, the phone cord ripped from the wall,
my body not mine. There were so many ways

to divide by seven—which year would be my last
there. The mountain air was a liar. The swallows
were liars, too. They came back, they came back.

They played in the sky, they dove, they sat on wires,
built nests on the porch lights, said with mud
and straw, *this is home.* I believed them—the flying

fish of them, their iridescence. The way they knew
the sky. This is not that place. I am alone
and not alone here, free. Sometimes the water

is a hollow—nothing to see but sea grass waving
and one white fish, so vast I am granular,
a speck, a nothing, and sometimes there is

everything—clouds of fish, threats threading past.
I may never find any way to love
and I may not *not* find any way to love.

I may, among the wrecked ships, the rusted husks
and split cable, find that I am the broken
dinnerware, the linens, my dead friends sent back

to find me in the half-light. Monsters and shipwrecks,
monsters and shipwrecks. I put my nose
to submarine cables reaching across the Atlantic

and whisker confessions out of them, answers
as inscrutable as the stars on the whale
shark's back, her mouth a cave I almost can't resist.

What I Have Lost at Sea

What have I lost at sea
        is a question you insist has an answer,
                the gap between flotsam

and jetsam begging the question
        about discarding versus truly losing,
                and while you explain that flotsam floats

up from inside and jetsam is
        introduced into the water,
                I think instead about generosity,

about walking into the bathroom
        at work and the paper towel dispenser
                has already begun its offering,

triggered in the dark
        to roll out its dry tongue
                before I open the door and switch

on the light, how one place
        where the dark is holy and offerings
                are made is not the sea, where generosity

is not a thing but beauty is:
        the octopus walking on two legs
                is beautiful, jet-packing away

or shrinking into a shadow it makes
        of itself, countless waving arms
                of anemones, the seahorse

that never seems to tip,
      the tiny fans in all the gills,
            the moray eels in caves, even the shark.

I think finding anything in the sea
      would be impossible. I am not at sea.
        I have lost everything here.

Cuchulain

Seven pupils in each eye—you find him planetary,
so many worlds to call home, and handsome

as a hand-tied lure skimming a river. Handsome as
a war, weapons in all our field uniform pockets, knives

in our boots, the way we kick in doors, our chests
barging in on families wide-eyed at tables. See him

by your hearth at night. You won't turn around
without making him angry—hair on end like pikes

in a pit. You are warned, *yes yes, the warp spasm,*
but what woman doesn't spend her youth saving men

from their worst selves—his one eye, the larger one,
fallen again in anger on his cheek, grape on a stem,

the other gone inside his head. Do not try to talk
him down—he can't hear you, will later talk and talk.

Still later, he'll rock you in his arms to bring you in,
singing Atlantic songs, Gae Bolga songs, the spear

made of bone—how it would never fail him—making
its one belly wound, but opening inside its enemy

into a dozen barbs loose in the rivers of the body,
the body needing to open to free the sword,

and you there, trying to be lost sight of as the night
wears on, thinking *yes, be a rock wall—yes, be gone.*

Objects in Mirror Are Closer Than They Appear

and what isn't closer than you thought?
Start with bills, so sweet over the transom
with the polite origami of their envelopes,
as if inviting you out of the house, out of doors,
away from your infernal typing: come, visit!
Until they come again. And again, closer and closer,
like texts from an ex-husband that you have cleverly given
his own ringtone—the science fiction one,
so that every time he wants something
he breaks into your village home like a flying saucer
landing on earth, so close, all of a sudden,
the peace and quiet you have built shattered,
and there he is, ray-gun brandished, demanding
what time, how much, why not, why don't you ever,
if you would only, I need to know these things,
if you want any money, you have to maintain
the spreadsheet, blaster, phaser, rocket-grenade,
the phone lighting up at night with him, lasers blasting
the bedroom blue. He is suddenly closer
than he appears so that all you want, since the first one
feels so small behind you, is another divorce,
a bigger one, like a shield. Anger behind you,
after all, is closer than it appears, and never stops following
like a small dog worrying the insides of his thighs
with small teeth while you try to sleep, the skateboarders
at night *clack clack clacking* down the sidewalk outside
the window louder than they should be in the village night,
when all else is still, or should be, leaving you to dream
of your daughter, who has gotten smaller, farther away,
sleeping in a dorm like a barracks amid piles
of impossible textbooks and labs,
this first few weeks bigger than you thought

when you stared down the barrel of time until she left,
for real, gone away what could be forever,
which is a really long time, considering what the mirror says,
whichever one is kinder, under the light of which sun
you have organized above it. Your face held there,
in various lights, you smiling, because that is what to do
in a mirror, smile in greeting as if you don't know
yourself—the sincere greeting for passersby,
the hello of myself, bigger than I know, smiling at others,
the lines of my eyes deepening so that I offer bird-feet
in greeting, the tufted spines of my plumage, gray,
growing downy, my neck bowed more than I know,
leaning studiously toward you, as if I care,
not as if now that is how it goes, bent,
looking closer into the mirror than I care to.

Portrait of the Family as a Definition

soon

From Old English *sōna* ("immediately, at once"), also, Frisian, Saxon, Proto-Indo-European. Archaic: right now. Has come to indicate the near future. Has come to indicate promise, as: it will happen.

1. Within a short period, a) At a time that is not long from now, as: *Soon,* said the Magic 8 Ball. The church bells ringing meant that another of his friends would be buried *soon. Soon,* we will all sit down to dinner. *Soon* after the last time they gave him the money, he came clean. Who knew how *soon* we would grow old? b) In a quick way, quickly, as: How *soon* can you help us? After you watch the boy through one-way mirrors, how *soon* will you understand? After dinner, we play with the Ouija board, but my brother is high and nods off *soon,* before we spell anything. How *soon* can you give him more money? I wish you'd told me *sooner.* It was too *soon* to know. c) In a short time after something happens, as: The window has been broken, and *soon* the thief steps in. When the brother is desperate, he says he needs food, and so, as *soon* as they can, the family gives him money. When the needle is inserted, *soon* the body tingles like sleep and the brother nods off. How did it get so late so *soon*?

2. Used to indicate one's preference in a particular matter, as: The mother and father would *sooner* do anything than forget. They would all *sooner* wait for a knock on the door than answer the phone. I'd just as *soon* forget.

synonyms: *any minute now, before long, in a little while, presently.*
antonyms: *after, afterward, later, never.*

My Mother Talks to Her Son about Her Heart

So what. So what that you grew
inside of someone else—
it doesn't mean you aren't in here now,
in here, right here. Oh, my heart—what's in here
is not all my own anymore, anyway.
There is Teflon, and stitching—other people's hands
have been in here. By this I mean to tell you
there is room. There is a house in here
I had hoped to fill. I saved clothes forever
waiting for more babies. So, I wanted you.
I always wanted you. A heart has four rooms.
You are one son. There is room.
When I was young and wanting to bring you home,
they found the hole in my heart and patched it.
I grow older and the outside door fails,
and so I get a new one.
In the lumberyard of the heart, the materials
are strange, Teflon, like I said, for the hole
and a valve from a cow to seal the doorway.
Over and over, I shore this place up.
Steady, old girl, I say to my heart,
and I call in its ticks to the doctor.
I love her, like I love you, like I have always
loved you. She calls me back and reads my stats.
I call your sister and tell her the score,
that I am always winning another day. *Steady, steady,*
ticks the pacemaker. I keep a good house. You know that.
These days, I keep my heart like a summer cottage.
The light is bright and warm. I won't speak
of anything else. You forget, you forget all the time.
You are supposed to come home. You are supposed to know
these things. You are supposed to know which door
to knock on, that I will open it.

In the Window at Áras an Uachtaráin

for Mary Robinson

When I was tall enough to reach the kitchen pull-chain
light switch, I figured it was time for me to know

where we came from. *Whist yer blether*, she laughed,
in her throat a hand of cards she wouldn't play,

the jar of pennies sleeping antes I stacked on the plastic
tablecloth while I ate lemon cake at Sunday dinner

and she bustled in a navy-blue dress, the paragon
of American grandmotherhood—I, a good girl who later

wouldn't listen. First, I was a farm wife who kept a house
of secrets. I was from nowhere. I failed and failed to make

my way. *What did I know of home*, I say sometimes now
as a way of lying to myself. I knew, and know, and if I am

to be honest now, I waited too long to learn to fight,
to talk back to myself like a light crowds out the night.

Street View

I Google where I come from in Ireland,
drag the yellow man into *street view*
and click the *spin* arrow over and over
so I can see it all. When I pull him off
the control panel, above his + and – ,
he flies, a patch of green hovering
below him, his own flying island, his little
earth shadow, smudged at the edges,
the earth-map ocean below pulling
at its beaches, my index finger's pad
the moon, my hand the god I am not,
though here in my village home, sturdy
and clapboarded, I am a kind of one
who can see across the world,
move a little man to where I want him,
spin him, and see what he sees, my Flex-Steel
Sofa and hassock my cloud bank god office.
If the phone rings, I will ignore it,
will hear the cars sighing through the village
like a lover sleeping, breathing in
and out like the waves on the flying island,
or the breathing of parlor pipes, the elbow
pressing its lung like fast-motion tides pull oceans
into plastic shapes, the peaks of them—
a god pinching a blanket into a fort.
He flies, and for a minute, because I can,
I flip him back and forth, dangle him
from his pivot head, his legs flipping
left and right, his arms back a bit,
like I am leading on the dance floor
and I have dipped him, the small of his back
arched, his arms not reaching out to save

himself—his feet no things for walking on,
his face no place for features. Then, the veins
of roads fill with blue, and if I drop him into one,
the earth will flip from *map* to *street view*
and I will see out of my man's eyes,
and where was he all my life? I walk
him around far out toward the bog land,
where Google shows so little green,
more brown as the hills climb toward
the border with Northern Ireland, stop shy
of the wind farm's five pylons, and I lift
my finger to drop him there, right in front
of the no-roof old house, which in map view
looks like a sheepfold, its roof long fallen
and rotted back in—a busted shoebox
full of derelict farm tools. I look for a way
to rebuild it, think five-gallon buckets
and some lime-wash, a new thatched roof.
I can do the metal kind myself, on my knees,
loving the world from above it, grabbing onto
the ladder to steady the vertigo, and though
he has no hands, I watch him scrape and smear
rough clay onto walls with a bullnose trowel,
each stroke burying perlite into the water
of the mix, the smoothest surface the one
longest touched. I can tell by the way
he does not look at me that soon he will
want me to start on the roof and the door,
and that while I have always been an insect
trapped inside a car, gone for a drive
that seemed a moment's thought, gone instead
to Florida, or the moon, the whole world
wrong once I was released, it seems that we
are a likely pair.

In the Harbor

I love the moment after buckling the seat belt
in a plane, headed God knows where—anywhere.
How I know there is no way to do laundry, dishes,
or fix a leak, everything all *fuck it* back behind me
on the ground once I've lifted off, which I think
is almost but also nothing like that moment after
the *Aquitania* has started moving, but first the smaller
boat in the harbor, which maybe I am on with them
when time happens again, starts to move, out to sea.
Last night we drank all night like I was the new dead
one, the stories told again and again like prayers.
When we are out to sea, we look back to see faces
ringing the shore like a fence, those we love in up
to their hips in waves, waving goodbye like mad.

Our House Behind the Hawthorns

Up the lane, each house abandoned longer ago
is deeper in bog moss and lichen. Our house

is just stone walls—a box filled with rusted bed-
frames and ploughs. Eleven children, two benches,

a plank table. Work and haul, kettle and hook,
stick broom, dirt floor, turf-light. At night, tiptoe

the edges of thirteen people sleeping. Come
morning, the clouds are what moves, the magpie

flashing like it is not afraid. The sheep say their words
with their heads low, as if they know a story

is a sacrament. What I came to learn: boxes have ways
of folding that children can't know. The man I called

Oh Goodness Sakes would tell me nothing—
signed the short song of his name with an X.

Work Song

Here is where I find myself, in a field of ghosts or letters,
where everything seems the start of a word or the start
of a fence, waves of grass like flags of *f* and *h*,
how whispers mean something else here, how sound
is measured out on a pillow, where people never go
to sound warnings. What rusts grows more beautiful,
doesn't it, steel a canvas slowly changed, oxidized back
to nothing. *Oh fence posts*, I always want to say, as if
to a lover, ever since I was young and riding in a car,
in my mind always on horseback jumping fences that flew
past. I keep fence posts in my heart, count days spent
digging them to mark a field—the digging bar I could lift
and drop, my shoulders heaving with a man not my husband,
the work easy to move through—the day like something
I had never known, like I could have whistled all the way
through it, nothing to drown a work song. I read fortunes
everywhere I can. There are days I see myself in mirrors
and windows, days, like this, etched on roofing blown across
the farm, my life ghost-painted there by what I have left.

The Woodpile

If it were your daughter you handed the logs to,
    in a line like a conveyor, one thing would stand for another,
stacking wood one way to know the past, where one thing
    becomes another, the shove of the shoulders and the pitch
of the hips a thing more like grieving than dancing,
    of giving something away over and over, landing it
with the precision of a triangle into an empty triangle,
    a curve into a swale, swing after swing, here and here,
your palms ending up up, a sign like submission, like *okay*,
    like supplication. I am not sure where it ends, this job.
No matter the cold, you are warm and no matter the cold,
    you hand her each log and she stacks it, you hand her each
log and she stacks it, the sound another variable, pitched
    between bell and knock. She is so sure of where things go,
here and everywhere. Somewhere in the day you start testing
    her, hand her the long table back at the farm, poultry feathers
everywhere, the pile of gravel that sat for years, the rusted baler,
    hayfields gone by, smashed plates, you hiding, you playing
this game until memory runs out and all there is is what was.
    You see what she does, see: no matter the cold, she is warm.
She moves back and forth, makes nothing of the dying box elders,
    their leaves no memorable shape. There is no taking stock.
She works with you like you are working, until you are finished,
    your backs bent the same.

In Leghowney, Donegal

My little grandaunt had no coat
and it lashed rain in March
on the way to school and the schoolmaster
at Four Masters saw her trouble
and sent her to stand by the fire
and the cold little girl in the wet dress stood
too long and dried the rain and caught
fire everyone running and patting
her out the degree of burns not anything
that survives in this story no other
details just the rain no coat
the teacher the fire patted out
the girl gone home to bed the girl
the pain and it was back then
so she died just like the cooper's wife
gone missing or the woman who was burned
in a pile of tires down the road a century
later gone a fire no cleansing
and nothing to do after but almost
get lost in time a woman I visit
saying no I don't know anything
about your family no wait I do

American Wake

The land is too small to serve all
and we must cross the sea.

Hold a wake for the living, the leaving. Stop the clocks
and turn the mirrors. Tell stories. Smoke and eat and drink.
It was never a question of whether they'd leave, but when.
Play games to pass the time—not to check that the dead
are dead, but to lift a lesser god. Tell what you've heard
about the New World. Later, all you will be able to tell
is what you remember. Let the keener loose on the night.
Let the house wail. Sing the songs. Let pipes keep evil at bay.
Square off with your child and dance. Let the neighbors
whose baby was born with a caul lend it—a charm against
drowning. Give dry cakes for the passage, a box of eggs.
Roast frogs, grind them to a powder, and bake into bread
to safeguard against fever. Take no shortcuts to the dock—
this is it. The bees will tell the otherworld who's gone.

The Magpie: A Key

One magpie means watch out.
One magpie in the yard means stay in the house.
Two magpies in the lane mean don't go farther than the roadside.
A magpie walking with its beak open, but quiet, means go out,
      but come home quickly.
A magpie calling means something will happen en route.
A magpie on the clothesline means watch your back.
Two magpies in the hedge mean don't worry about what the sparrow
      that hopped inside your open door means.
A magpie flying, or a tiding of magpies, means place large bets
      against tomorrow.
A tiding of magpies spotting the sloped field means the old man
      up the road is lonelier right now than you are.
A magpie on the fence means leave the mail in the box.
Two magpies, one flapping its wings, mean yesterday was better
      than today.
A magpie landing in the dooryard while you are looking out
      the window means your systems are working. Steady on.
A magpie mentioned by a neighbor who stops by means
      what you said first made poor sense.
A magpie pecking at the gravel means work harder on how to speak
      after long silences.
Two magpies walking together away from the house mean draw
      the curtains and the door. Something you don't know
      is on its way.
A magpie under the rhododendron means you have not hurt anyone,
      or questions and answers have come apart.
Two magpies in the old garden mean choices are long shots.
A magpie, two magpies in a rough wind or rain mean making
      anything, or minding anything, is a slow race home.
Two magpies on the stable roof mean the days have packed
      their bags.
One magpie making a nest has stolen what you love.

When My Brother Dies

It happened already. It has happened five times
    and will happen again. My brother is dead.
        We try to recover what he stole and start
           by making a list we can't finish.
I've been living up and down the same riverbank
    since I started having families. I stay on my
        side of the river, which makes our list full
           of half-truths. I will not cross the river.

They try to cross his hands across his chest,
    but the hands keep falling. My brother's skin
        is older than my dead uncle's love for bees
           and sunlight, my uncle in the sunlight in his trailer
saying, *they want me to leave, but I love it here,*
    spending days in the hallway once, fallen.
        My brother seems to love the satin sheets,
           his hands falling to touch them again.

When I lean my hands on the fancy wood,
    I slip my brother a lollipop with a violet inside it.
        A sister is supposed to put something into the coffin
           to show love. So many nights we sat by the TV
while he pawed a bowl of candy, nodding,
    nodding and scratching at his face, his neck,
        as if plants had bitten him up. I don't know
           how to tell him what it means to live on a river.

I don't know yet that he will die again. The ice
    lets go on the river and floats away like pool toys
        piloted by tiny children. Rivers fold into themselves,
           like oars into water, like little boys hurt too much

and I want to tell the tiny children, *be careful,*
    but there is no time to grow to love them
        as they braid downstream. I walk home uphill,
            past the comfrey and the massive oak.

In the john boat, my brother and I float and row.
    Water weeds skim the boat. We eat quartered
        oranges and lean our backs against the gunwales
            and rip worms onto tiny hooks. We forget
what is coming and act like there aren't
    any more deaths to come. We are lazy.
        The water moccasin coiled under the seat
            keeps its mouth shut as we climb out.

Which death are my parents crying about
    now? I wonder if it's motorcycle death, or locked-
        in-jail death. I hope it's shot-by-a-gunman death
            and not wasted-away death. Hypodermic needle
death is the one I know it always is, though. It's a blue
    and translucent death, this time. We cry like our eyes
        are needles, the plunger pressed. We cry like sugar
            water and dirty apartments. There he goes again.

Here is another ice rink, another red-faced
    olly olly in come free. I am telling on him again.
        He's dead again and look what he did, look
            how he won't wake up. Where does he keep
going? He never packs a thing. The dog
    eats the linoleum and his son shakes him
        to wake up, little *daddy daddy,* jabbing
            his father on the brown couch. We say,

He won't wake up.
        It's a game it's a game?

his son asks and we say, *no*, or practice saying *no*.
This brother whose first parents disappeared
like ghosts, this father who keeps dying
on couches and in vans knows how to do
this one thing, this laying back of the head,
this wooden blanket from the waist down,
this wooden blanket top door closing.

Homegoing

I.

The stone in my prodigal father
is ancient, a holy place, his hand
holding these roses like the slate roof.
I have been asking this farm
to bring me home tied to branches,
to bottle roses. The river never saw me
in bed asking how it prays,
or said: carry this pen back home
to bless home—water is never shed
from a kneeling back. Nothing falls
there like a watch in the quiet,
hung by a string to the wall,
the cow asleep. The ghosts I find
would empty the lakes of bones.
They tell the nail to bend like my mouth.
Show me if I would grow inside
a bottle. In my father moves
the cattle he never knew.

II.

In the cattle shed there is a bottle
tied to a string, hung from a nail
in the slate stone wall. Inside is holy
water, to bless the cow. I have never
been to this farm, never knew lakes
like this, or saw my father find the bottle,
bring me back to show me, tell me
he prays it never falls. Nothing moves
in the quiet home by the river. Asleep,
I watch my father bend his bones
like the roof to the ancient roses,

asking how to hand-carry the branches
home, kneeling, asking if these roses
would grow in a bed back home.
I said they would, my mouth empty
like the holding pen, a place
of prodigal ghosts.

The Dead

They worry I won't keep the graves when they're gone.
See my mother brushing off her hands

at her mother's grave, surveying lots,
approving and disapproving care and neglect,

my father deep in thought. The trees above
them are the gods of Massachusetts, big-

handed and quiet, tall fathers approving
the play of children in the yard. Somehow

the graves meant new stories about who was buried
underneath, our dead becoming more real,

not only more gone. When I walk with the dead here
in my village, I want them to say more than their names

and relations, lambs on children's stones, more than
the dates that must mean influenza, or some

illness that doesn't kill us anymore.
I don't want to walk the rows anymore wondering

what shape stone I want, which says more,
the obelisk or the square, marble or granite,

and am I the wife of someone, or am I not.
I want something to happen here, some kind

of story. Maybe the little ghost from my house
will pick up her dress and run to show me her name,

or a flood will wash away the riverbank
—and a knot of bones. Or, slow motion, a hand

will work its way up through the grass—something
the graves can do to us, the way they trip

me when I walk over them, the soil a bit
lower where they have settled, these long dead

I can play whimsy with, unlike the dead
my parents will be, unbearable and new.

If They Mean to Have a War, Let It Begin Here

My brother can't swim. No promise of shipwrecks
can make him keep a needle out of his arm. I tread water
out past the dock. Our mother makes piles of rocks, twenty-eight

rocks in each, rocks for years. If you put your hand between
her shoulders, her back is a shell. Our father paces and remembers
the Revolution, its many dawns like holidays. We only want

to take a vacation. We want to get away from home. Other
families do it and return refreshed. We have come to John's
Pond as a last resort, to regroup. We only want

what we can't have, each of us striking off. Every direction
we take is grace. My brother's teeth fall out one by one
like casings as he sings about the whites of our eyes.

Work Song: Ruin

The thatch roof like a hillside field
is mended by the man who crawls its back
stitching new thatch over fissures
made by sun and water while a fissure
somewhere else is not stitched.
Who can keep up with the rate of mornings
breaking the county into lean harvests,
every roof a field of grass
bent under rain, bent down as far
as the nearest resistance, and under the roof
it is the floor of packed dirt
like the square field under rain.
In my photograph, they stand in the doorway,
the house a squat white width
of stone, the roof a thickness of thatch.
The man crawls, darning holes
in the roof, while the hayfield is not tedded,
the man on the roof not baling hay
while the weather clock ticks its warnings,
the hillside field waiting, already
cut in this race against rain that falls
cold in needles and sheets. My children
lean over sills to see the hearth,
anything but ghosts. He bends
on the roof like he shears sheep, his forearms
driving shears like a tractor through hay,
dropping fleece into hillocks like garments
piled high for mending, the woman
having had enough of mending. They will
have enough of mending. Imagine
that they have. Send him on a ship to work
in Liverpool, send her walking

five kilometers to the village
and home, alone, for what the farm
can't make by itself, these gears
turning like a millstone grinds
barley into malt, this kind
of alchemy, children scattered,
lime-wash worn off walls given
to moss, roof straps soft and grass
growing through the dirt floor.

Longshoreman

Shoulder to the barrel, weather sturdy,
the taste of the word *wheelbarrow*
when you ask to borrow your neighbor's
because you don't have one.
See also *rigger—horsepower*, force of will
against the barrel's will to object.
Longshoreman: a thing to holler from deck
to put men in line on shore—*along shore, men!*
Shape up, a thing to do to get hired,
to wait in a clump in the morning
to be hired, pie caps snapped, rolled,
pocketed, sweaters, wool pants,
skin weather red, breath a kind of exhaust
—a crowd of chimneys craning
above morning, a pallet of grandfathers.
The ships exhaling, inhaling men
and goods, their voices threading
through foghorns and rigging, clanging
like unregulated brokers, their eyes
giving a go at the classifieds after work
in an easy chair, grandmother in her chair
nearby. Negotiate sling loads.
Deal in dry goods, tally pallets, rope the stacks
in place, hold steady sheaves and sheaves,
lock down goods in the ship's belly.

Joke

You walk into a bar, look at the TV. Benedict is stepping down.
Say to your friend, *No Pope?* Friend says, *No Pope, radio,*
and laughs. Other people laugh, too. Worst nightmare—
a joke you don't get. Pretend you get it. Later, look it up:
absurdist humor from the 40s—two elephants in a bathtub,
one asks for soap, the other says, *No soap, radio.*
In the 40s your father learned the butt end of a joke
was Italian, their thumbs on market scales in the North End,
your father's father flicking his hand at them to back away
—the competition, who might beat him to the docks,
houses to paint, your father's father lugging stepladders
and paint buckets on city buses. A joke was a way to kill a man
who was after your living, not a luxury of soap and elephants.
You know who you are from what you understand: a joke
a place to hide, a suburban neighborhood, where your white skin
hides your immigrant family, where a joke is no luxury
of absurdist landscapes, clocks melting, dripping, or men
standing around wondering whether to hang themselves,
waiting for their God. People begged for work in your landscape,
in other people's homes and kitchens, in shipyards, cargo
piled to load, men with arms like masts—people with no idea
how letters worked, fled to this country, where other people
built worlds out of them, out of what you could not understand.

A Hagiography

Heads will roll, we say when shit gets bad,
but they don't anymore—no more Saint Alban,

his head rolling downhill into a well, the water
turning holy. No more Saint Eluned, her head

rolling downhill into a stone from which springs
a healing well. Ditto Saint Winifride, beheaded

by a suitor who wants her, but she loves God,
her head rolling downhill, up springing a healing well

where it stops—but swift Uncle Saint Beuno
reattaching her head—but still, she was ready to die.

Where was Saint Denis going when he walked
downhill into Paris, holding his head in his hands?

Where does anyone go with their head in their own hands?
And what sermon does he give, this man gone walking

and praying, having played chicken without backing down
from men with swords, scourged and racked?

What is there to say? When I walked into his Sacré-Coeur
and walked a circle around its stations, I had nothing

to say. The sumac that grows along the highways
where I live catches me, driving past—its branches'

slowest-motion dance, the prayer of its reaching—
its berries an extra stretch toward the sky's

fine blue ceiling, the sumac a patient whirling dervish.
I walked my Sacré-Coeur circle, past its saints,

thinking of the trash mound of its foundation,
the cathedral stretching up, away from Paris,

my face wet because I wouldn't die for any kind
of faith—the not-even-sumac reach of my heart.

On Interstate 89 North

I don't know how close I was.
I was not paying attention to him

or his raised middle finger, which
he was tired of holding up,

his face lowered out the window at me,
glass down, even though the air

was freezing in northern Vermont.
I have sped past, unthinking, it's true.

I have sped past so many things.
How many miles until I know what I have done

is always the question. For a minute,
I thought I should be afraid

and watched him in my mirror in case
he sped to catch me. I have sped past and have been

unthinking so many times I want
the world to know. Once, a man leaned out

a passenger window and fired his gun at the sky
as I sped past. One time, a deer jumped

across my hood, which was accelerating,
while my son and I belted out,

Why do you build me up (build me up)
Buttercup, baby

just to let me down—
and nothing was the same afterward.

He grew, next, into someone
I'm desperate to track, to keep from harm,

to follow into the underbrush, wearing
orange vests or branches, depending.

The man crouched down in his fast, small car.
He stayed in line and left the highway

without closing his window,
which was when I knew I was still alone.

A sign: one semi-truck cab hauling identical cabs
—one climbing up on the next, identical.

I know I was not wrong.
The way each carried the next, as if knowing

there was no other way to go.
And each was precisely like the other

so I craned my neck as I sped past them, too,
in case they, too, were astonishing.

Nest

The robin flaps between the box elder and her spring nest,
hopping up and down one branch near our back porch
where we drink coffee and talk about her poor choice
for a home—on the fire escape, the door to which is open,
an exercise class blasting music inside the grange hall.
Winter is finally done and our firewood tarp is drying
in our back yard, under the tree. We make the small talk
and silences of morning then hear a dull sound. *I think
that robin just laid an egg on the tarp*, he says. My *No*
meaning nothing to the blue egg at the edge of our ocean
of tarp, its mother high above it. *Oh no*, I say, but he goes
to get it, ambling across the yard, the egg a mote in his hand.
When I protest, *she'll abandon the whole nest*, he walks up
the escape to put it back, telling me quietly, *it's a myth*.

Aubade with Heavy Equipment

after Neruda

We wake to Johnson Paving Company's trucks
bringing our new tar, the morning full of steamrollers,
the driveway freshly covered while we are away at work
between morning and your steadfast interruptions

over our screens at night, where you are a ramshackle shelter
inside which I have signed the guestbook and every document,
deed, license, flight plan, agreement you put in front of me,
each of which I send to all recipients I can imagine, saying, *yes,*

I love you, over and over, without decoration or corsages,
without instruction manuals and without analysis. I wait for you
to come home from work soon, or, you're sorry, soon, or not soon

enough, and despite my clothes on the floor so close to wreckages
you will not name—your hand steadies my back as I fall asleep,
a shortcut, so few miles as the crow flies that I might dream.

Passerines

I want to tell you about the thud at the back door,
      that my man says, *bird*. That later we see its tail
      sticking out from underneath the siding. That its
      tail-feathers shine like oil, shifting purple to blue,
and we are kneeling on the wet decking. The yellow
      of its stomach making it something more
      than the brown birds everywhere, a tiny prize
      for kneeling there, for prying back the vinyl siding
to find a yellow-bellied flycatcher, its cheek bloodied.
      I want to tell you how he held it, said, *passerine*
      before it took flight. Little passerine. Songbird.
      Before she left, I brought my daughter to St-Jeannet.
There were swallows like boomerangs near dark,
      like here, like everywhere I go. I want to tell you
      about the neighbor, the scientist, who said they were
      swifts, not swallows. Swallows are passerines,
but swifts are not. *Passerine*, I had thought, *passerine—*
      a more future verb tense for *to pass*, a tense I can't
      know yet—a passing I can't understand. The order
      of passerines is a mess, the scientist said. It's impossible
to track their evolution. I want to tell you I don't understand
      evolution, any of it, even mine, becoming the mother
      I will be next, the one who lets go. Once, I stood
      on a bridge and a man taught me to call sparrows to eat
from my hands, told me he was a sinner, that what he did for me
      was atonement, which is a thing I might understand.
      I want to tell you there is nothing like their tiny grip,
      the way they quiver while they peck at your palm,
wanting to fly out of reach. I want to tell you what happened
      when I let her go, but I don't understand it yet. I want
      to talk about this morning, the little yellow bird in sudden,
      dizzy flight. The trees full of yellow. How I lost sight.

One Way to Apologize to a Daughter
for Careless Words

At Station Island, I am hungry for a beehive cell,
seeing purgatories under each mound and statue.
    There is walking to be done, circuits of trying to fall
and catching myself over and over, a way of moving forward
    I have practiced for years. At Station Island,
I am a penitent, which means I have sinned, but also means,
    if I wish, that I have words to correct. The *penitent*
is the word that corrects the one used earlier.
    I regret, for one, telling you, at the Wayside Diner,
that you don't belong. Here, I forgo speaking.
    Fifteen hundred years of us coming here to apologize,
the air never warm enough, and if I had walked here
    from the farm, I would have walked miles with no roads,
the reasons I have come as un-chartable as yours
    for the things you do. You walk the old man Walt around town,
reminding him of the world, and I come across it to go home
    to this place, to say what words between us
could not accomplish. All over Ireland, there are rowboats
    at lakes to bring the penitent to islands. The water here
promises drowning—guernseys knitted to know fishermen
    washed ashore from the sea, but nothing like that for the lakes,
the families crossing together. There is no way to recognize
    a family that has drowned. When we have had enough of land,
we cross water, glad for the lurching of it—our bodies glad
    of the unsettling. How else am I to weigh all I've done?
I cross in some kind of silence, given the birds' and the oars' complaints.
    I shouldn't tell you this, but I take my shoes off for you.
I remember how to love statues, the way they hold
    their palms up, their shoulders back. I eat nothing.
Three days in, I say your name out loud.

How the Heart Works

I keep thinking about the way the heart works,
but I think about it wrong, on purpose, the way
I do other things on purpose that I shouldn't,
like one-click shop for books that wait for me
like dogs in cardboard coats until I come home
for them and let them in. No, I keep thinking
about the heart, the one my mother has.
There are all kinds of words for it, words
her doctor says, words she repeats to me
about what's wrong with it. I see her, on the phone
tied to the wall by a coiled cord, the doctor
blue-toothed on the other end, telling
her what is happening inside her rib cage,
the one I keep seeing like an ornate birdcage
someone has planted a tiny-leafed ivy
inside, hanging in the corner, or at the edge
of the fireplace, on a tiny table, long spindly legs
and a top as small as a book, not as the housing
it is for the heart that does all kinds of things wrong,
things I can't know, no matter how many times
the aorta of it is repeated, no matter which
carotid phone call ends in semi-lunar
valves, there are always left and right atria,
greenhouses of the heart, the tricuspid valve-way
opening onto the patio my father has turned
over, stone by stone, so it looks new,
and pulmonary arteries growing like
hydrangea, there, outside the glass ventricle.

My Brother Wailing

There is a river outside my window, which is more
than I ever asked for. Sure, a river is a bigger monster
than I am used to, but, most of the time, it is no worse
than my brother. The river stones get worn fine,
like my parents did. All of this is more than I asked for.
Even the armchair by the window. I didn't ask for that
any more than I asked for the word *soon* to mean
what it does. *Soon* is everything, almost. My brother
was almost a mountain. Not in the way that mountains
are majestic, but in the way that mountains are also monsters.
He blocked the sun often enough, even from himself.
What is a boy to do in the armchair—with the tourniquet
gone slack, his veins filled with the drug I always thought
must feel like sugar tastes—but let the light fade?
This is also what mountains do, they let the light fade early
in the houses to the east of them. I remember my father
pinning him to the stairs, himself a mountain, and my brother
wailing, like he did not understand. My father was a mountain
in the way that mountains are mountains, tall, majestic, proud.
My father was a mountain in the way that mountains greet
the morning, like a basket to hold the sun. *Good morning,
good morning*, the houses to the east filling with light.
The people sit on their porches and watch. What the boy does
on the other side of the mountain is he becomes a river,
and soon, and he does what rivers do, he becomes a monster.
He etches and etches shadows into everything. I rescue his dog,
who has eaten the kitchen floor. I even rescue my brother once.
Monster friends come to visit. They smile and they have diamonds
in their teeth. I get a gun. I tell my parents to get a gun,
but they are mountains. They carve a path against the sky instead.

Worry

I make all the plans in the world, all the lists.
The sink, never empty. Nothing is ever done.

My eyes have been trained on empty birdfeeders.
I walk or think of walking and am already tired

of gardens going by—the tireless work of neighbors
walking dogs, walking babies, doing yard work.

Every houseplant goes brown before it is watered.
I study not-doing, or worry, like a craft.

My mother taught me to worry, for instance, about
heart attacks. I feel them coming all the time.

And when mine comes, one minute nothing, the next
minute upon me, one minute watching birds in the trees,

who will go through my things and what will they find?
Every day I wonder, in large groups of people,

why nobody is dying. If more people die in private
than in public, I wonder, how fabulous the chances of living

if I stay in groups? A positive outlook also helps,
I keep telling my mother, or she keeps telling me.

I married the man of my dreams from the get-go,
I start by saying. There was not a care in the world.

The Big Dig

The games were *Hide-and-Seek*, *Horse*, and *Chase Paul*,
whom we couldn't catch—my brother a *DNC*, secret code
for *Does Not Count*, and we meant well, that he could play,
that his mistakes wouldn't count, but this is the story
of how he kicked the ball for all he was worth and didn't
make anything happen, how he ran from sewer to sewer
like his life depended on it, how he followed us around,
red-cheeked, while we made the baskets and hid in the bushes.
What am I to say? That all is forgiven? That the milk
is in the milk box on the back porch? That the neighbor boys
didn't mean it when they tied him with a garden hose
and threw him in the pool? That I never held the knife
in the night kitchen air? That everything was worth it?
Listen, the books we read were *Are You My Mother?*,
The Little Engine That Could, and *The Monster at the End
of This Book*. What else is there to say? That at some point,
after the last time he came clean, I believed him?
That I understood addiction, before it was too late,
as just another illness? That I became, as he became,
a good person in the end? That when I visited him
at his apartment next to Logan Airport and did not say
what I felt, that I felt forgiveness? That when our mother
told me later she was missing some cash, I didn't have a steel
heart, that I felt a sparrow of regret (said, instead, *I am never
going back*, and *Jesus Christ*, and *that fucker*)? Soon after
his son was born, I dreamt I met my brother at a laundromat.
His hands were skeins of wool and he couldn't work
the machines—like a brontosaurus with a fork. His union card
was tucked into his cap, and next to him on the floor
was his jackhammer from the Big Dig. It was my last chance
to get things right, so I took my twenty paces
and we squared off like two cowboys across the cracked

linoleum. My gun was a mouth that could not stop yelling,
and he just stood there, empty as a stolen child, not even
this dream big enough for the two of us.

Choose Your Own Adventure: Loneliness

1   I'm lonely, you say to the wall
at night in the village. You forgot to pull
the shades and you feel even lonelier
with the world so big around you.
5   Pretty soon, you are really small
from all the thinking about the universe
that happens there on the red couch,
your knees up under your chin by now.

          to get up and get a snack, continue to line 9
          to get even smaller, go to line 18

The cupboard with the peanut butter
10   and graham crackers is really, really far away,
35 feet, by your estimation, and you reason
that this is closer than most of the things
you were just imagining, like asteroids and
gaseous belts and undiscovered civilizations,
15   so you go get a snack, flipping light switches on
as you go because it had become dark
while you were thinking.

          to run out of snacks, go to line 32
          to disappear, go to line 43

Your knees are like two mountains,
the kind that sheep graze treeless,
20   and you look at them until they are
mountainous, and you are still looking
down at them, because you are flying
over them in a single-engine plane, a two-seater,
but you are alone. People looking up

25 can't see the temporary sunlight
    flashing against your wings' aluminum.
    You are curious about clouds
    that are coming in from the ocean,
    mountains and clouds, and you, the little
30 speck people can see from below as a kind
    of cross whining overhead.

            to give up, continue to line 32
            to find meaning, go to line 40

    There is nothing here, you think,
    exposed as you are, and alone, as if it is
    a kind of portent. The map flipped open
35 nearby tells the way to many
    places, none of which feels possible,
    no dot on the horizon any better
    to arrive at than this. Be hungry
    if you want. Nothing will fill you.

            to give in, end here
            to take a kind of stand, continue

40 After flying over the mountains
    of your knees, you consider shrines,
    how still they are, the human monument.
    You spend a little lifetime as a shrine,
    a limestone woman holding
45 her son on the side of the road,
    fenced in for safety, so no one can
    take him from you (like your ex-husband
    just did), where the visitors and the curious
    consider you less than they do themselves,
50 their offerings not really for you, anyway.

Homing

The sky is at the feeder again.
I mean the indigo bunting
with no bearings for home.
A man pulls into the driveway

after work—crunching stones,
hallooing up the stairs—
wanting to know about my day.
All the days are wranglers,

I say. I am not able to cite
my sources, but I make a list.
A woman at lunch said we do not
plan to live two hundred years,

and so I think to tell him
—well, I do not plan to live
two hundred years! In my hands,
pillowcases I bought, embroidery

floss. Everywhere I go I think
about what is impossible.
Can homing pigeons carry
their nth letter and still get lost?

My job is to build a home,
I tell this man I have already built
a home with. My job is to do
something with my hands.

At Franklin County Airport

Here there is no air traffic control, just a quiet radio.
You tie down your plane and sit inside at the table
where I write. I learn about near misses from you.

Even when I tell you I have to work, you tell me
the next story—or call over to the other guy, saying,
Frank—it's true, right? You remember. You bite into

your sandwiches like heroes. I think of the swans
up the road, scrabbling inside their wrought-iron fence,
as if this town were the center of anything, as if a case

could be made by anything here for swans, for a town hall
replica for them to shade inside, swans at the center
of this place where people fall off the edge of the earth,

walk away from their homes and never come back.
Some of us up north have no idea where we come from,
no idea what might come. Once here, we risk losing

ourselves, losing children in the school with no windows.
At dusk, here in the airport, I watch the sun go down
and wonder what it's like underneath the flat earth

spreading away from me. The roots of all of us dangle
in the dark, shrink back from the sun while we sleep,
our bad dreams pulled back inside the darkness,

our children running amok to find their edges. I wonder
what the swans have to do with anything, why I always think
about them fenced inside the green, inside the rotary,

cars driving circles around them, their beaks sifting water
and mud, everything they do making circles, their beaks
hammering the earth soft, their feet packing it down.

Night comes and I watch the trees fade. I remember
the time you pointed out the satellite, your arm
a pointer I couldn't follow. Yes, I said, I see it,

though I didn't, and now, waiting for you to finish work,
the snow comes down like a single bedsheet
over the north. I hold the swans out like a question

I can't answer. I don't know what they mean
any more than I know how to lift one of these small planes
off the ground, but I know the growl of their engines,

that standing behind one, its prop wash will knock
me back. Years ago, a woman ran out to her husband's
plane to ask him for something, and the propeller,

still running, invisible as insects' wings, cut her down
as fast as we swat flies. Some god must have felt
like we feel then, taking aim. I wait for you to lock

all the doors and check the tie-downs out past
where she died, out past where you turned the door
into a wall no one could walk through again.

You check and check every lock and undone thing.
The chair I love best faces the old door's frame, just
under the sheetrock, proof of nothing, of where we go.

Getting Ready for Bed

Yes, I have cleared the signals off the dresser
and keep sweeping auguries from the oak floor.
What are we but a scroll of worries? I keep
gadgets not needed for any tragedy—
tape measures and screwdrivers for everything.
I sing songs to the red chest of tools in the garage,
thanking them for safety. We always laugh,
going headlong—*Life and limb*, I said, *life and limb*,
when we got married, the pig behind the barn
starting to brown. We kissed tongue twisters
and answers under the disco ball upon which I insisted.
Take your medicine, I think, while I brush my teeth
every night standing on one foot. You think I'm ridiculous.
I never tell you the crane is a symbol for long life.

Saying the Rosary, Station Island

The words are here as we are, just arrived. I don't know
who says the rosary, for real, out loud, like this, like an engine

loud enough to fear, my chest hot with it, the priest beginning
each beaded decade like daily announcements hardly made

of words. I didn't come for this, but it takes me, and soon
I am walking outside, around and around the chapel, the priest

droning another decade, all of us walking in a circle, around
the chapel, past the lake, the holy water font, past the restrooms

where the Dyson hand-dryer joins the droning, a little engine
of extra prayer, the men and women exiting the restrooms

sad cheaters, penitents come back to say their prayers, walking
the stones around the church, with a dozen priests arrayed

and praying with 500 penitents, and me, and my father,
and my cousin, and my son. And at my feet, so help me God,

is a photograph of the new Pope, which we have brought
to have blessed. And when the time comes to bless it, bless all

the things in the church, the hundreds of things at people's feet,
we will hold them up while the priest—whose last day is today,

who will cry as he wishes us goodbye at the end of our eight hours
of praying—masses and rosaries—says a new prayer, and we hardly

know he has changed to a new kind of praying, so we almost miss
the blessing. I keep studying the light fixtures, rather than my father

or my cousin—my son having moved up front to sit alone, confused
by all this, not having been raised in any church, but also walking

into it with his chin up, the only child here, giving himself over
to this new apparatus—if I look at their faces, their open mouths

saying things I only ever said in my head, or in a place like this,
which is a place I have never known, if I look at their faces

again, I'll fall apart on this little island in a lake over the hill
from our family farm, which took us almost a hundred years

to return to, just across those hills, where two black-and-white
sheepdogs wait in the shed room for us to come back.

Awake

This morning I bramble toward waking—
alarm alarm alarm snarling my dreams like little girls
around a pile of marbles arguing *quitsies,*
no quitsies. This morning I don't know. This morning
I am lagging with my dead, reminding them
they have already gone first. I knuckle down on the day,
make strides and comebacks. I ride a train
and write and keep crossing out the word *rather.*
I never know what I want until afternoon
and sometimes trim the walkway instead of thinking.
I pull the curtain on who I am, keep shame
for my sleeping like a terrarium of whistles. Somewhere,
someone finds me phenomenal—I stand
so tall and keep the future as a pet. Together we swim
the headwaters like children who don't know
the rules. I forget who is playing for fair and who for keeps.

Late Winter

The river sends smaller
and smaller floes of ice

downstream, crocus making
their way up. Rocks are inside

my shoes by the time I'm home.
Five winters now I run my hands

under your shirts, start at the top
to split the buttons from their catches

and end the cold. My hands make a set
of wings under the placket.

Moth or hawk,
I don't know which I am.

Moving Again

We could make a mobile out of bromeliads, I say,
looking up at our new high ceilings, and my son asks,
what's a bromeliad? I tell him they don't need soil
or water to grow—they take what they need from the air.
We have just moved to this neighborhood where lawns
and appearances have to be kept up. The platters
are stacked in their narrow cupboards, and his father, again,
is raging at a distance. I remember when possibilities
felt endless, when summer lasted like a great illness.
I lower the windows so the summer rain doesn't come in.
My son helps, pausing to smell the metal screens for their
correspondence. Soon, he will make his own homes.
He stops to clarify—*they don't need anything? No,* I say.
They eat the air. They can make home anywhere.

Nine White Deer

for Sarah

The sea forgives nothing on Inis Oirr,
though I think it might, outnumbered
as we are by stones and bees,
the campanula suggesting *stay,*
playing their purple bells in the wind.
The cell and church stand open
to the sky like mouths and what might be
square tombs show their backs.
Gobhnait ran from her family's fighting
to live here in a stone cell no bigger
than a rowboat, underground,
next to her church—a church so small
we think it's a ruined cottage at first.
Barely legible in the grass beside it,
the stone outline of another room
where the coffee and doughnuts were served,
we laugh, shushed by a woman who points
through the narrow door at a priest
in white robes, his arms up as if to hold
the sky, the church roof gone. We stand
with our palms to the stones and listen,
feeling the thinness, eyes welling.
We are waved in, given a book,
sound out words in Breton and guess
the melody of "Heureux,"
our textbook French barely a guide,
not even the carline thistle's gold
readying us for the communion we take,
the wine we share across time. Halfway back
in time until Christ a vision told Gobhnait

to leave this place—not to settle
until she found a herd of nine white deer.
There, she would find her resurrection place.
I know how tired she must have been.
A double hawthorn tree stands like a mother
at the top of the meadow, shark fins
and bird bones hung from her branches,
skulls tucked in her elbows.
I leave a shell at her feet with a prayer
for my family, walk out
past a square white stone covered in moss
and broken shells, where the birds
break snails for their meat.

My Broken Family

My broken family was a cooper in old times,
knowing units of measure better than most.
My broken family learned the trade of keeping things in

like shipwrights learn how to keep water out.
A barrel floating, a bottle with a ship in it, and a message
in a bottle were all the same to my broken family.

To calm my broken family, I leave scraps in the yard,
in an old bowl under the box elder. My broken family
doesn't like to beg, but it likes the edge in my voice

when I walk my dog after dark, so tired from everything
I just want to sleep. My broken family doesn't like it
when I forget. The sand that gathers after rain

at the end of my driveway is my broken family's
calling card, saying things like *remember* and like *once*.
My broken family is the railroad-car ferry on the bottom

of Lake Champlain, its captain delusional from gout
and morphine. Dive to see my broken family.
Keep my broken family out of it, I say to people who ask,

but it can't leave me alone. Once, I gave my broken family
a mason jar with holes in the lid for air. Once, I put it
in a shoebox with a nest. I fed it what I thought it needed.

Forgetting

Forgetting a day, days, feels like learning how to see
—how the hooded crow at first can't be seen

but scatters at the sound of footsteps, sudden,
like flying boats headed nowhere, seen landing

together nowhere on the mountain that has no name
on any map. I am learning (in the slow way I made

my way back here to where I'm from) to think about
my bones the same way Ruth Stone thought about hers.

Here is what happened today, or what I can remember.
A man said, *I could murder a cup of tea,* when he walked in

from the sheep and the rain. I made tea the same color
as the river falling through the rhododendron. Let us

let go of stories—learn to see but not remember. In half
or less of my life, none of this will remember me at all.

Killeter Forest: Father McLaughlin's Well

We cut through the forest to check the sheep
on the far mountain and stop to fill our bottles.

Sitka spruce make a grid filled with moss.
Above the holy water, on a shelf, this shrine:

baby toys, wrappers of pills; prayer cards;
Star Wars posters; Jesus, his beard chipped,

pointing to his flaming heart; next to him,
another Jesus, broken ankles, alabaster,

hollow and full of leaves, a hole clear through
his chest; baby dolls, a cane, and facedown

there another Jesus slumped beside the shotgun
shells, packs of cigarettes, snow globes.

Near inhalers and Hello Kitty and zipped baggies
of jewelry and charms, another Jesus, hands open.

We kneel to bless ourselves. Midges worry
the air until they find us. Nearby, in the asphodel

in the wet ditch, horse bones almost clean
look like what I think I am underneath.

Under the Bluestack Mountains

Around every corner is a man with a dog
and a shepherd's hook. When the coast is clear

I wander into old homes, their doors hanging
loose or gone, and try to tell myself the story

of how it all ended, of who was the last to go.
I look under a mattress. I scan shelves, hearths.

Sometimes I think I am home. When the rain stops,
I walk, naming what I know: *fuchia, holly, rowan.*

Three years in, I'll stop asking what everything is
and learn in secret: *chaffinch, magpie, hooded crow.*

We lived under Cruach na Míol—stack of midges,
stack of beasts, of the cattle and the whales.

I put supper scraps on a post for the birds and fall
asleep in a place so dark nothing has a beginning.

Shaking the Sheets

The rain skims Cruach na Míol in visible waves
until it's my ghost aunt shaking the sheets

to smooth them, though she knows already
that she is getting nowhere. I make tea and stay in,

the collie running in his sleep on the linoleum.
I let the days waste away as if I have not come

across the world to be here, as if I might ever
know the difference between work and rest,

as if the woman whose house this was would
not turn me away, as if I have found my place.

I weigh what I thought against what I know—
let the morning disappear as if disappearances

were kind, as if a windmill were some kind
of measure. I stay until the fuchsia come and go

in the hedge and rowan berries grow inside
the ruined house. Some days, I don't know

what happened—by which I mean I don't know
where the days have gone. At night I can't sleep,

as if it is my turn to shake the sheets. As if I know
more than I should, and she knows that I do.

Planetarium

I roam the antique shops in town to outfit
our new house, bringing home two flying saucer

lamps, a silver bracelet with a blank field
for a name, and a vintage Nova Home Planetarium

to surprise you—thinking you would be someone
who had one as a boy—and set it on the dresser

in our bedroom, giddy to show you. I unpack
a few boxes, poking around the house like an

adventurer who doesn't believe in booby traps.
My mother calls to say my brother has overdosed

and is gone. Her voice is a long and terrible song
that grows a crack in my chest. Or my bones double.

Our home becomes a replica of a home, twice as big
as a place I can call home, then collapses flat.

I make some necessary phone calls. Friends come
to sit with me in pajamas and listen. That night,

in bed, I stare at the ceiling and tell you every story.
I walk you back with me. I expand, too. I want

to know where he is, really, *where*? I have asked
so many times now, Where *is* gone? You get up

as if to go to the bathroom or some other mundane,
dark-of-night, glass-of-water chore, and I think

no, not now, but you turn on the planetarium
and light up the sky so I can see where he is.

Losing

My brother is lost. I can't find my brother. I say it over again—
when I lost my brother. A back road I knew once and now

can't find. A specific wave on John's Pond. The last one we saw
there, the blue-lipped sleep of overdose. He goes from one

office to the next, and no one will return my calls. One day
he was somewhere. I know he must have been. The difference

in weight between alive and dead. Do the old experiment again.
Weigh the escaped soul. Let it have gone somewhere. Let it

have packed one bag. Is my brother any amount of atoms at all,
fending for themselves? If I keep saying, *I have lost my brother,*

is there a corollary? Do I make way-finding? A compass,
a geocache, a crashed plane on his island, his black box full

of laughter? Every next syllable said by everyone is my brother.
Silent mouths—these are where dead brothers live. I keep

a jar of nails like a bouquet of denial. Life ends with us finding
leaves underfoot. Fend for ourselves, I'm saying. There is music

everywhere. There must be a bit of his breath left. Put the needle
in the track again. My brother, somewhere, knows the tune.

In Event of Moon Disaster

*from Nixon's alternative speech in case
of a failed moon landing, 1969*

The mother should telephone
the constellations
to find her son.
This is a burial at moon sea.
Others-to-be will follow
into the unknown,
and whoever looks up at the moon
prior to prayer
will remain foremost
in a state of under-mending.
There is no recovery
for their hope.
In ancient times,
our heroes looked at stars
and saw our hearts stirred in.
Families should adopt
the same procedure.
Nights to come,
the brother, in the corner
of another world,
will send for friends.
They will stay on the moon
to rest in peace.

Mass General

They've put the television on
for my brother, wild horses
grooming each other four stories

above the streets of Boston,
my brother oblivious to horses
and the hurricane warnings

across the bottom of the screen,
storms more massive now than ever,
super storms like monsters

crashing through fishing villages
—the storms named for us,
in alphabetic sequence,

so that we are the eye of ourselves,
watching our own landfall,
for instance a shadow

comes across the breakwater
which is my sisterhood. I am
no longer a sister.

My brother is dead—his tight Mohawk
just a path now to follow
with my fingertips, his mouth

taped shut—his body hooked up
to every machine, him long
above the room, looking down,

his EKG scroll curled on the window
sill, my mother into my father, into me.
His heart will be transplanted

into another man's chest this week,
my father telling everyone
at the wake where his son's heart

has gone. We watch the horses
nick each other's necks and ask
questions. No one knows

what to do now, so we stay
in room 8 for too long, standing close
as people come and go.

We watch the horses.

reverse overdose

my brother's heart is transplanted into a stranger
machines keep my brother's organs alive for days
he is declared brain dead my brother's hand is so warm
I think he will wake up I sit and hold my brother's hand
I rush to the hospital my brother's lips are blue and he's not
asleep his roommate calls 911 she thinks he is asleep he falls
off the wagon he buys something for the pain he tells
his roommate he needs to go meet a friend desperate men
swap heroin for fentanyl she heads out to the clinic
his neck hurts all the methadone is out of his system

it's morning he's a good dad he rides his bike for miles
to see his son every weekend I try to get him into a shelter
but he can't afford the train across the city to the clinic
he comes clean I try to save him when he's homeless once
he comes clean he rides his bike to see his son the summer
he loses custody or his wife kicks him out because she's
into someone else his wife kicks him out because she is high
he comes clean they have a baby boy they are high and low
high and low high and low a photo of him as the handsomest
man I've ever seen I don't recognize him he comes clean

he marries a beautiful junkie he's high all the time a photo
of him with dreadlocks and a sheepish smile at christmas
he invites friends with gold teeth and guns to the woods
where we live he runs out of food but won't ask for help
he comes clean I bring him to live in the woods with me
I try to bring him something in jail but nothing is allowed
he misses my wedding I save his border collie he goes to jail
for selling 40 pounds of pot in a suitcase our father reaches
for his garden shovel men come to my parents' front door
looking for my brother we watch *snl* while he is high

his dog eats his garbage and the linoleum in his apartment
and shakes he steals our grandmother's silver dollars
he breaks in through our windows and skylights and takes
our stereo and whatever else our parents kick him out
he grows pot in his closet and our parents call the cops
a photo of him in a neck brace at a dead show his afro in the sun
doctors bring him to the quadriplegic ward so he can know
he's lucky doctors fuse a piece of his hipbone to his spine
he breaks his neck but doesn't know for days his dirt bike flies
over a cliff he delivers the early newspaper with our dad

he hates hockey our dad plays hockey so he plays hockey
too I find him on the coffee table driving the zamboni between
periods of the bruins games he squeals when loose puck
is on the ice yells *dad loose puck is playing* I hear him
in his room saying *body of christ amen body of christ amen*
I lie and tell on him for hitting me a photo of him in a flowered
ski coat and fireman boots and hockey stick I ask my parents
for a lock for my bedroom door he tells me he came from
a dinosaur egg I ask him where he came from what his name
used to be we have a homecoming party for him in the back yard

a photo of him waving on the picnic table wearing a bow-tie
and a bow on his head we bring him home red-cheeked
and blond he holds my fingers and tries to walk I meet
my new brother on boston common my brother saves our mother's
life I visit my mother and swing from the bar above her bed
my mother has open heart surgery doctors find a hole in her heart
during the pre-adoption exam the agency wants to make sure
my parents are fit to parent I eat canned spaghetti sandwiches
on wonder bread when they visit social workers visit to make sure
we have a good home my parents apply for a new baby boy

Only Child

I wake to the train whistle saying, *what you don't know
might hurt you*—with nowhere to ship the stories
I keep to myself. Somewhere in the middle of me
they link end-to-end, blowing their whistle into steam
in the cold air of things I know that I wish I didn't.
My mother is the engine, pulling the cargo down the line.
Secrets hop from one car to the other—and some losses
—a brother and a sister in the graveyard up the road
from my house, both named Baby, and two others
never buried. I have a brother on his way there, made of ash.
I know more about him than he ever did. *Don't tell,*
we often said, *keep this to yourself.* I go back in time
to quiet my brothers and sisters. I sing apologies to them.
I hold them close. Forklifts can barely lift what's left.

Weeks After My Brother Overdoses

I search Craigslist for *sadness*: a white couch the only result.
Happiness lands red shipping containers, and that's it.
I wander through days like an envelope marked *please forward*.
Listen. My brother is a ghost. I keep thinking *I am not a sister
anymore*, though others assure me I still am. *Just sister them*,
builders say to make a thicker beam, or to span a distance,
join the faces of two-by-sixes with nails, make more from less,
make do. No one will let me have my sadness or tally
what I've lost. I make lists like recipes for how to go on alone.
I draw his death when I doodle, making little crime scenes,
as if this epidemic were a murderer, a suspect, a criminal.
I draw him on every sidewalk to inflate the numbers, to give
my brother to everyone. Inside the outline, I do some math.
I add him to seventy-two thousand and subtract him from me.

Epistle: Joyride

It's a nice day for a ride—bright sun, clear roads,
two of us headed down to Cape Cod to see your son,

my own boy riding shotgun, his playlist keeping us quiet
so I can turn to you, try to hear you better. Car rides
make me think of us when we were little, always fighting.

Remember the waffle prints the vinyl made on the backs
of our thighs, how the VW held on to our skin in the summer

when we tried to move our legs? Remember the Maginot
line down the middle of the back seat, our fingers threatening
to cross it, the other one whining or yelling, our parents

yelling back, *stay on your side or we're going back home!*
—or making up games, you the master of Ever Who Sees—

always seeing the Sagamore Bridge first on the long drive
to the Cape. Nothing to fight about now. We go from one
mundane adventure to another, you in your little urn

at the bottom of my pocketbook—shopping, visiting friends,
to work and home. I open my pocketbook, and there you are.

I wonder how it is, being gone. We were at a basketball
game, my son playing, your son watching, or maybe it was
the game before. Anyway, mom said, *here, open your bag,*

amid the boys yelling *ball ball ball* and the sneakers making
complaints against the floor boards and the smell and haze

of sweat, the Zero Gravity complex alive with boys, and she
handed me your ashes, wrapped in Kleenex, wrapped in
a sandwich baggie—the portion of your ashes I was to have,

to keep and to bring back to Ireland, to our family farm
or find your family farm—or crossroads or forest. There's

a whole Ireland of possibilities, another place you've never
seen. Today, though, this blue sky and this thread of cars
winding through the woods of New Hampshire. My son

has brought everything he can think of to entertain your son,
let him know there is joy, that there's a way forward for

every little boy. Next to me he slouches in his long body,
lithe and strong, freestyling, telling me about his life, the one
he is building away from me, as he should, sturdy, solid.

You have no idea how many basketball games you've already
been to with me to watch him, how many burgers afterward,

how many hotel rooms in search of the perfect game.
You know, I think that game is for teaching young men
how to suffer disappointment, how to be told by grown

men that they are wrong, that they can't do what they
are doing, that they can't talk back. They fight for something

that doesn't matter at all. They go to the floor for it.
Maybe you can hear me. I talk to you in my head now,
ever since the sparrows came to my windows the day after

mom called to tell me you were gone. You are as quiet as ever.
I drive this car like it's a church for the living. I tempt everything

that could kill us—bridges, boulders, sometimes shouting,
Not today, rock! My son tells me I'm not funny, but I know that.
I won't squander this day, every song on Spotify seeming

to tell me something about you. Are you here with us?
Your face lights up here, underneath Boston, in the tunnel

you built. It's good to see you proud, clear-eyed. The light
is good today, too, isn't it? This car goes fast enough that
we can joke about everything. The "Central Artery/Tunnel

Project"—were they kidding? Did they love a cruel joke?
You in the middle of it, my own Central Artery problem, veins

a network of trial and error, like this city, now beautified.
Do you remember those little red spiders back home?
How we smeared them on the concrete to see the red lines

they drew? Or popping the hosta buds in the rock garden—
how mom never knew, and they would never flower. So much.

So much. I am still your sister, you know. When people ask me
if I have any brothers or sisters, I still say yes. No more yelling,
no more reconciling—nothing more we can do, little brother

of ash at my hip—I don't know how anyone scatters someone
they love. I don't know how to hold what's gone, either.

The greenway above us, its carousel, the grass the children
play on now—there is at least no more worry. This bridge over
the Charles reaches down with God's fingers to hold the road.

Kingfisher

The speck of island across the water
          has its heron, and, farther, dairy land climbs
away from the lake where the cows lie down.
          Perch bones line the shore. *Looks like rain*, we say,
but not even the rain will come, no hummingbirds.
          Nearby, the kingfisher points its beak at the lake,
the air full of lake-water—silver on silver,
          how the world looks in drops of mercury,
parabolic mirrors, daguerreotypes. Like cancels like.
          I tilt my head and each is the other. Nothing moves
the wind-chimes. On the railing, a fish skeleton
          like an x-ray against the cedar, bones lit up like nothing
else, mouth-hinge open, eye socket looking up—
          the slack mouth saying what the eye socket sees.
All the shoreline bones nearly dry, leathered over,
          little spines pointing in every direction, that tiny look
of terror in the mandible: there is nowhere to go.
          The kingfisher calls its failures, empty beaked,
most of the time, and waits. No boats go by,
          no eager kayakers, not tomorrow's armada
of pontoon boats, not even the woman who stands
          on a paddleboard and gondolas herself all over
the lake, dipping her serious oar on either side.
          Just the diving kingfisher breaks the bowl of the day,
wing-beats uneven, wings rattling, hovering, wings
          breaking the dive, telling me what I already know:
What's done is done. There is nothing left to weigh.

Ashes

After he is gone, his birth sister calls, finally thinking
she has found her brother, too late to meet him
for the first time. I can see his face in hers, his sweetness,
as if I have always known her, as if she is my sister, too.
She brings his birth mother's name and birth certificate
—what he had never known, names and dates, keys
to his past, and I spend the summer hunting for where
he came from, ancestor by ancestor, as if they could
do anything to make amends. I search as far as I can,
until records disappear, to find a place to lay his ashes,
to bring him home. I want to find his coordinates.
Everything unbelievable happens. Locks open. I promise
to keep secrets. I stand in Old St Peter's graveyard
under the church tower, in a pocket of graves walled
inside the city, under a brand-new mural of warrior Rory
Og O'More and Margaret O'Byrne and their wolfhounds
breaking into the day, the painted giant and his wife
standing watch over the unmarked graves of Portlaoise
and over me, holding my brother in my hand. A light rain
falls, and the woman who secretly let me in waits out
on the sidewalk, telling me to take my time. Here is where
my brother's dead must be, or here is the ground where
his people gathered for centuries, or here is a horse chestnut
tree that has to be four hundred years old that his people
must have seen, so there I stand, with him, telling him
he is home. I let his ashes fall through the ivy growing up
the largest tree. Because we never know what to do,
because I will never see him again, I fill my raincoat pocket
with the tree's conkers. In the game of Conkers, children
thread them on strings and take turns swinging them,
trying to break the other's conker—a game we would
have played if we could have, if these trees had grown

near us, growing up. A conker that has never beat another
is a *none-er*. If two *none-ers* compete and one breaks
the other, it's called a *one-er*. I'll keep going up the country
to Donegal, to the bridge over the river at the crossroads
to Meenadreen, and after a week of carrying the rest
of the ashes back and forth into the mountains, will put
half on one side of the bridge where the water eddies
peacefully and half on the other side where it falls over
rocks through the rhododendrons into a tiny cave of a valley
and pools there secretly, visited only ever by my family
—the only ones who know it's there, until I'm finished
dividing my brother into halves before my flight home.

Home on Holiday

in Laghey Village

A gas station clerk asks if I'm home on holiday
when he hears my accent, flat as a stone
in me, gone as long as I've been—forever I'd say
if home were a place I had ever been before.
When he tries my accent, dull as bone,
then I think I know what he means
—as if home were a place I had been before.
I am a map of work and names from way back
when. I finally understand that he means
I've been turned around. To find home
I worked my way back from a map of names.
I rent a house where I'm home already, bring
what I've found of me—what I thought was home
in me, gone as long as I've been, forever it seems.
I rent a home where I'm home already, begin
at the gas station. I tell the clerk where I've been.

Acknowledgments

Sincere thanks to the editors at the following journals and publications in which these poems first appeared, sometimes in different form.

Academy of American Poets' *Poem-a-Day*: "Epistle: Leaving"

American Poetry Review: "Objects in Mirror Are Closer Than They Appear," "Only Child," "Street View"

Beloit Poetry Journal: "Passerines"

The Collagist: "The Dead," "How the Heart Works"

Four Way Review: "Late Winter," "Homing," "On Interstate 89 North"

Horsethief: "On the Moon," "My Broken Family"

Los Angeles Review: "reverse overdose," "Weeks After My Brother Overdoses," "Awake"

Love's Executive Order: "A Hagiography"

New England Review: "The Magpie: A Key"

Pratik: A Magazine of Contemporary Poetry (Nepal): "Moving Again," "Shaking the Sheets" (under the title "The Rain"), "Work Song"

Ploughshares: "Losing"

Prairie Schooner: "When My Brother Dies," "Killeter Forest: Father McLaughlin's Well"

Sixth Finch: "In the Harbor"

SWWIM: "What I Have Lost at Sea"

Tinderbox: "The Woodpile," "My Mother Talks to Her Son about Her Heart," "Portrait of the Family as a Definition"

A number of poems in this book also appeared in the chapbook *Keep This to Yourself* (Button Poetry, 2020).

"Passerines" and "The Dead" were reprinted in *Roads Taken: Contemporary Vermont Poetry*, edited by Chard deNiord and Sydney Lea.

Gratitude...

To the National Endowment for the Arts, the Vermont Arts Council, the Sustainable Arts Foundation, the Vermont Arts Endowment Fund, and the Vermont Studio Center, whose support helped make this work possible.

To Tony Hoagland, Rodney Jones, Maurice Manning, C. Dale Young, Debra Allbery, Ellen Bryant Voigt, and the whole community at The Program for Writers at Warren Wilson College for invaluable support and guidance.

For reading this manuscript in progress: Didi Jackson, Major Jackson, Matthew Miller, Elizabeth Powell, and Noah Stetzer. And for working on poetry together: Ben Aleshire, Eve Alexandra, Jari Chevalier, Penelope Cray, Kristin Fogdall, Gabriel Fried, Maria Hummel, Matthew Lippman, Holly Painter, Dawn Potter, Alison Prine, Meghan Reynolds, Brad Richard, Jennifer Sperry Steinorth, Emilie Stigliani, Tanya Stone, and Bill Stratton.

To Adriane Little and Spencer Brownstein for filmmaking magic.

For poems that inspired some of mine: Natalie Diaz ("When My Brother Dies"), Cecily Parks ("Homegoing"), Adrienne Rich ("Seal Bride"), and Matt Rassmussen ("reverse overdose").

To Rachel Willey for gorgeous cover art and to Tammy Ackerman for making this book beautiful on the inside.

To Joshua Bodwell at Black Sparrow Press for faith in my work and for every careful step in bringing this book to life—thanks for every single thing. To everyone at Black Sparrow, I owe so much, happily.

To my parents, for bearing with me and these poems; to my children, Cal, Emma, and James, for the richness that is my life; to my dear husband, Cliff, assistant to my imagination. To my family in Ireland: Pat, Philomena, John, Eileen, Caroline, Liz, and Jade; Mary and Eddie, Mike, Kelly and Rosemary, and all the rest, for taking me back in.

Photo Jess Dewes

Kerrin McCadden's debut collection, *Landscape with Plywood Silhouettes*, won the Vermont Book Award and the New Issues Poetry Prize. Her chapbook, *Keep This to Yourself*, was awarded the Button Poetry Prize.

McCadden has received a National Endowment for the Arts fellowship and the Sustainable Arts Foundation Writing Award. Her poems have appeared in *Best American Poetry* and the Academy of American Poets' *Poem-a-Day* series, and in such journals as *American Poetry Review*, *Beloit Poetry Journal*, *New England Review*, *Ploughshares*, and *Prairie Schooner*.

She is associate director of the Conference on Poetry and Teaching at The Frost Place and associate poetry editor at Persea Books. She teaches at Montpelier High School in Vermont and lives in South Burlington.

Printed February 2021 in Quebec, Canada for the Black Sparrow Press by Marquis. Set in Elena with Gill Sans for titling. Interior design by Tammy Ackerman. This first edition has been bound in paper wrappers for the trade; 26 copies have been lettered A–Z and signed by the author.

Black Sparrow Press was founded by John and Barbara Martin in 1966 and continued by them until 2002. The iconic sparrow logo was drawn by Barbara Martin.